THE SECRETS OF BREAST CANCER BATTLE

OVERCOME THE DIAGNOSIS, MAXIMIZE SURVIVAL CHANCES, EMBRACE HOPE AND HEALING, AND ACHIEVE LASTING EMPOWERMENT

DR. PREETAM JAIN

ABOUT THE AUTHOR

Dr. Preetam Jain, MD, DM, ECMO, is an eminent Medical Oncologist and consultant at leading hospitals in Mumbai, India. With over 15 years of experience, his journey is marked by **academic brilliance, unwavering commitment to patient care, and outstanding contributions** to oncology, particularly in breast cancer treatment. A gold medalist with distinction, Dr. Jain has earned multiple awards, including the **Healthcare Excellence Award, Excellence in Oncology in Indian Health Award,**

Outstanding Young Achievement Award, and Social Impact Award.

His book, **The Secrets of Breast Cancer Battle: Beyond Diagnosis, Maximize Survival Chances, Embrace Hope and Healing, and Achieve Lasting Empowerment**, reflects his dedication to providing knowledge, hope, and empowerment to breast cancer patients and their families. **Driven by a deep sense of compassion** and a personal commitment to improving patient outcomes, Dr. Jain's approach combines cutting-edge medical science with genuine empathy.

His dedication to his craft and his commitment to helping others look and feel their best have earned him a reputation as one of the most trusted and respected **Medical Oncologists** in the industry. **Looking to the future**, Dr. Jain remains committed to advancing cancer care, with the goal of improving not only survival rates but the overall quality of life for his patients. His patient-first philosophy ensures that every individual receives the best possible treatment along with the emotional and psychological support needed throughout their journey.

In addition to his professional achievements, Dr. Jain has a passion for traveling and is known for his exceptional oratory skills. A keen cricket player and an avid socializer, he delights in connecting with friends and colleagues. His active participation in social events and networking opportunities highlights his innate charm and grace, making him a charismatic presence both personally and professionally.

CONTENTS

INTRODUCTION TO BREAST CANCER

Understanding Breast Cancer

Breast cancer is the **most common cancer among women** worldwide. It is a cancerous tumor that typically manifests as **a hard lump in the breast tissue**, resulting in uncontrolled growth and multiplication of cancerous cells, which might spread to other parts of the body. Breast cancer is a **complex and multifaceted disease** that affects millions of individuals worldwide. It is also the **leading cause of cancer-related deaths worldwide** in women, especially among older adults. The overall incidence of breast cancer is notably **higher among women of higher socioeconomic status**. Early stage breast cancer is highly treatable, whereas women presents at late or advanced stage are associated with significant morbidity and mortality rates. Understanding the intricacies of breast cancer is crucial for healthcare professionals, patients, and the public. This book will explore the various aspects of breast cancer, including its **different subtypes, risk factors, and treatment options.** The positive news is that breast cancer is highly treatable and curable, especially when diagnosed at early stages.

It is essential to recognize that **"ALL BREAST CANCERS ARE NOT SAME".** Breast cancers are classified into various subtypes. When you consult your oncologist, they will first assess the type of breast cancer and then determine its stage.

To aid in understanding, it's important to know that three major protein receptors are expressed in breast tissues:

1. **Estrogen Receptors (ER)**
2. **Progesterone receptors (PR)**
3. **Her-2 neu protein expression**

Breast cancer classification is based on the presence or absence of these hormonal receptors and HER2 protein expression:

1] Hormone receptor-positive breast cancer

This is the **most common subtype**, accounting for approximately **65% of cases**. Estrogen and progesterone receptors on cancer cells characterize it. Hormone receptor-positive breast cancer is treated with hormone therapy, which blocks the effects of these hormones on cancer cells.

2] Triple negative breast cancer (TNBC)

Triple negative breast cancer **lacks hormone receptors** and **HER2 protein**. It is typically **more aggressive** and challenging to treat, particularly in advanced stages. **Treatment options** may include chemotherapy, targeted therapy, immunotherapy, and surgery.

3] Her2 positive breast cancer:

The **expression of the HER2 protein** characterizes this aggressive subtype on cancer cells. HER2-positive breast cancer **grows rapidly and has a higher risk of relapse**. The development of **targeted therapies**, such as trastuzumab, pertuzumab, and ado-trastuzumab emtansine, has significantly **improved outcomes**. Treatment often involves a combination of surgery, chemotherapy, radiation therapy, and targeted therapy. Ongoing research continues to explore new treatments to enhance outcomes.

4] Inflammatory breast cancer

A rare and aggressive form of breast cancer, inflammatory breast cancer is marked by **redness, swelling, and warmth** in the breast. It is typically diagnosed at **a later stage** and requires **aggressive treatment**, including chemotherapy, surgery, and radiation therapy. Early detection and treatment are crucial.

5] Hereditary breast cancer

Individuals with a **family history** of breast cancer may be at increased risk. **Genetic testing** can identify mutations in the **BRCA1 or BRCA2 genes** associated with a **higher risk** of breast cancer. Healthcare professionals should be knowledgeable about genetic testing implications and how to counsel at-risk patients.

In summary, understanding breast cancer is vital for healthcare professionals and patients to facilitate early detection, accurate diagnosis, and treatment. By educating ourselves about the different subtypes, risk factors, and treatment options, we can work together to improve outcomes for those affected by this disease. Patients should consult their oncologists to stay informed about the latest advancements in breast cancer research and treatment to receive the best possible care.

Common Risk Factors

As previously discussed, breast cancer is a **multifaceted disease** with various risk factors that can increase an individual's likelihood of developing the condition. **Understanding these risk** factors is crucial for effective **prevention, diagnosis, and treatment**. It's important to note that many women diagnosed with breast **cancer may not have any** identifiable risk factors.

Age is one of the **most significant risk factors**. The likelihood of developing breast **cancer rises with age**, particularly for **women over 50** or those who are **post-menopausal**. The lifetime risk of developing breast cancer is **approximately 1 in 8 women**. However, it's essential to remember that breast cancer can also affect **younger women**, especially if they have **a family history** of the disease.

Genetic predisposition is another **major risk factor**. Certain gene mutations, such as **BRCA1 and BRCA2**, are known to significantly **increase the risk** of breast cancer. Women with a **family history** of breast cancer or other cancers should consider **genetic testing** to evaluate their risk profile.

Reproductive history plays a role as well. Women who have never had children (**nulliparity**), experienced early menstruation (**early menarche**), had **late menopause**, or gave birth at **a later age** may have an increased risk. Women who **did not breastfeed are also at a higher risk**.

Benign breast disease with histological features, such as **hyperplasia with atypia**, is associated with a higher risk of developing invasive breast cancer.

Lifestyle factors also contribute to breast cancer risk. **Obesity, lack of physical activity, and alcohol** consumption have all been linked to an increased risk. Long-term use of hormonal replacement therapy following menopause has also been associated with a higher risk of breast cancer.

By **recognizing these common risk factors**, individuals can better understand their own risks and take preventive measures to reduce their likelihood of developing breast cancer. Proven preventive strategies include adopting a healthier lifestyle, undergoing regular screenings, and considering genetic testing where appropriate. These measures can help **mitigate the risk of breast cancer and improve overall outcomes**.

The importance of Early Detection

Early detection of breast cancer is vital for improving patient outcomes. Identifying breast cancer in its initial stages allows for **more effective treatment** and a **higher chance of successful** recovery. Regular screenings, such as **mammograms** and clinical **breast exams, are essential for detecting** breast cancer before it has a chance to spread to other parts of the body. Healthcare professionals play a crucial role in emphasizing the importance of early detection to patients and encouraging them to take part in routine screenings. According to recommended guidelines, **all women over the age of 40**, who are **at average risk** of developing breast cancer, should undergo **screening mammography annually**.

Early detection guidelines from the National Comprehensive Cancer Network **(NCCN) classify breast cancer screening** into **two major categories** based on risk:

Average Risk Women

- **Ages 25 to 39**:
    - Clinical examination every 1–3 years.
    - Breast awareness education.

- **Ages 40 and older**:
    - Annual clinical examination.
    - Annual screening mammogram.
    - Continued breast awareness.
    - Consider supplemental screening for women with heterogeneous or extremely dense breasts.

High-Risk Women

High-risk factors include:

- **Lifetime risk** of breast cancer **≥20%.**
- History of **radiation therapy** to breast tissue between ages **10 and 30**.
- **5-year risk of invasive** breast cancer **≥1.7%** for individuals aged 35 and older (as per the Gail Model).
- Atypical ductal hyperplasia **(ADH) or lobular** neoplasia with **≥20% residual lifetime risk**.
- **Pedigree or family history** suggestive of or known genetic predisposition.

For high-risk women, screening and follow-up should include:

- **Clinical visits every 6–12 months,** starting when identified as being at increased risk. Referral to a genetic counselor may be necessary if not previously done.

- **Annual screening mammogram**, beginning 10 years before the youngest family member was diagnosed with breast cancer, or at age 40, whichever comes first.

- **Annual breast MRI,** with consideration for contrast-enhanced mammography (CEM) or molecular breast imaging (MBI) for those who cannot undergo MRI. Whole breast ultrasound may be an alternative if other imaging methods are unavailable.

- **Risk reduction strategies** and continued breast awareness.

For patients, understanding the **significance of early detection** can **empower them to take** control of their health. Proactively seeking regular screenings increases the likelihood of detecting breast cancer at **an early, more treatable stage**.

Education about the benefits of early detection and routine screenings is crucial. In developing countries and low socioeconomic communities, social taboos and lack of awareness often delay reporting of breast lumps, leading to diagnoses at advanced stages and compromising survival rates.

In summary, the importance of early detection in breast cancer cannot be overstated. Patients should recognize its significance and take proactive steps to **ensure early detection and treatment.**

Chapter 1

TYPES OF BREAST CANCER

1] Triple Negative Breast Cancer

Triple negative breast cancer is a subtype of breast cancer characterized by the **absence of three key** receptors: estrogen receptor (**ER**), progesterone receptor (**PR**), and human epidermal growth factor receptor 2 (**HER2**). Because triple negative breast cancer lacks these receptors, it does not respond to hormone therapies or HER2-targeted treatments, making it **more aggressive** and challenging to treat compared to other breast cancer subtypes.

This subtype is more commonly diagnosed in **younger, pre-menopausal** women. For healthcare professionals, it is crucial to discuss the distinct characteristics of triple negative breast cancer with patients to ensure they receive the most appropriate treatment and support.

Triple negative breast cancer **spreads rapidly** and has a higher **likelihood of recurrence** after treatment, underscoring the importance of early detection and aggressive management. **Chemotherapy remains the primary** treatment for this subtype, as hormone therapies and HER2-targeted therapies are ineffective. However, patients may also benefit from emerging **targeted therapies** and **immunotherapies** that are currently **under research**.

Oncologists should support patients with triple negative breast cancer by **providing comprehensive information** about their diagnosis, treatment options, and potential side effects. Given the **aggressive nature** of this cancer, patients may experience significant emotional distress and anxiety. It is essential for healthcare professionals to offer psychological support and resources to help patients manage the **emotional challenges** associated with their diagnosis.

In summary, triple negative breast cancer presents unique challenges that require **specialized treatment and compassionate support**. Healthcare professionals play a vital role in **educating patients** about their condition, providing effective treatment strategies, and offering emotional support throughout their cancer journey.

2] Hormone Receptor-Positive Breast Cancer

Hormone receptor-positive breast cancer is the **most common subtype**, representing approximately **70% of all breast** cancer cases. This type of cancer is **defined by specific** hormone receptors—**estrogen receptors (ER)** and progesterone **receptors (PR)**—in the cancer cells. These receptors are integral to the growth and proliferation of the cancer cells, making hormone receptor-positive breast cancer both distinct and treatable.

Prognosis and Treatment

Patients diagnosed with hormone receptor-positive breast cancer have a more **favorable prognosis** compared to other breast cancer subtypes. This is because the cancer cells depend on hormones like estrogen and progesterone for their growth, allowing them to be effectively **targeted by hormone-based therapies**. The **primary treatment** approach is hormone therapy (also known as **endocrine therapy**), which works by blocking the effects of these hormones on the cancer cells.

Diagnosis and Management

To ensure accurate diagnosis and treatment, **hormone receptor testing is essential**. This process involves analyzing a sample of the tumor tissue to identify ER and PR. With a confirmed diagnosis of hormone receptor-positive breast cancer, healthcare providers can design **a treatment plan tailored to the specific needs of the patient. This personalized approach** enhances the effectiveness of treatment and improves patient outcomes.

Advancements and Future Directions

Recent advancements in the treatment of hormone receptor-positive breast cancer have been promising. New and innovative therapies, including **targeted treatments** and **combination therapies**, have been developed to further improve patient outcomes. Ongoing research and clinical trials are continually exploring **novel treatment strategies** to advance the management of this subtype of breast cancer.

Summary

Estrogen and progesterone receptors on cancer cells characterize hormone receptor-positive breast cancer, accounting

for approximately 70% of breast cancer cases. This subtype typically offers a **more favorable prognosis** because of its responsiveness to hormone-based therapies, which block the effects of these hormones on the cancer cells. Accurate diagnosis through hormone receptor testing is crucial for tailoring effective treatment plans, which often include hormone therapy.

Advancements in treatment, **such as targeted and combination** therapies, have improved outcomes for patients with this subtype, with ongoing research continuing to explore new strategies. Understanding hormone receptor-positive breast cancer is essential for healthcare professionals, patients, and caregivers to ensure **optimal care and enhance quality of life**. Effective collaboration and communication are key to managing this subtype successfully and making strides in breast cancer treatment.

3] HER2-Positive Breast Cancer

HER2-positive breast cancer is a subtype characterized by the **HER2 gene**, which encodes a protein that speeds up the growth of cancer cells. Representing about **15-20%** of all breast cancers, HER2-positive breast cancer is more prevalent among **younger women** and is known for its **aggressive** nature. These tumors are typically **of higher grade** and have a greater tendency **to spread beyond the breast**. Without intervention, HER2-positive cancers are associated with higher **recurrence rates and poorer prognoses**.

Diagnosis and Treatment

Determining **HER2 status is critical for guiding treatment** strategies. HER2-positive breast cancers are initially tested using **immunohistochemistry** and fluorescence in situ hybridization **(FISH) on biopsy samples**. Treatment usually involves a combination of chemotherapy, surgery, and radiation. **Targeted therapies**, such as trastuzumab and pertuzumab, have significantly **improved outcomes** for this subtype. These drugs specifically target the HER2 protein, effectively inhibiting its growth-promoting effects and enhancing survival rates.

Advancements and Impact

Introducing **HER2-targeted therapies** has revolutionized the management of HER2-positive breast cancer. Prior to these advancements, HER2-positive breast cancers had lower survival rates compared to other subtypes. However, with the **use of HER2-blocking drugs in combination with chemotherapy, the prognosis for patients with this subtype has markedly improved**, bringing it in line with outcomes for other types of breast cancer. Ongoing research and treatment advancements continue to enhance the prognosis for this aggressive subtype.

Summary

Despite the challenges posed by its **aggressive nature**, HER2-positive breast cancer has seen substantial **improvements in treatment outcomes due to targeted therapies**. Identifying and accurately treating this subtype is crucial for achieving positive outcomes and improving long-term survival. The **evolution of HER2-targeted treatments** has given many patients better chances for a **favorable prognosis** and **reduced risk of recurrence**.

4] Inflammatory Breast Cancer

Inflammatory breast cancer **(IBC) is a rare and aggressive** form of breast cancer, representing **only 1-5% of all** cases. Unlike other types of breast cancer, IBC rarely presents as a palpable lump. Instead, it is characterized by **redness, swelling, and warmth in the breast**, often **resembling an infection** or rash. This atypical presentation can **complicate early diagnosis**, leading to **delays in treatment** and potentially poorer outcomes.

Diagnosis and Treatment

IBC is known for its **rapid progression**, often spreading quickly to **nearby lymph nodes** and other organs. **Early and accurate diagnosis is crucial for improving treatment** outcomes. Because of the aggressive nature of IBC, a multidisciplinary approach is essential. This involves a **co-ordinated effort among** oncologists, surgeons, radiologists, and pathologists to develop and implement a **personalized treatment** plan.

Treatment for IBC includes a **combination of chemotherapy, surgery, and radiation therapy**. Neoadjuvant chemotherapy is commonly used to shrink the tumor before surgery, which can enhance surgical outcomes and reduce the risk of recurrence. For cases with **HER2-positive** tumors, **targeted** therapies such as trastuzumab and pertuzumab may also be used, providing additional options to manage this aggressive subtype.

Challenges and Support

Despite advances in treatment, **IBC remains challenging** to manage, with a **higher risk of recurrence and lower overall** survival compared to other breast cancer types. Patients with IBC may also face significant psychological challenges because of the disease's aggressive nature and its impact on physical appearance. **Comprehensive support is vital**, including access to counselling, support groups, and resources to help patients cope with both the physical and emotional aspects of their diagnosis.

Summary

Inflammatory breast cancer **is a rare and aggressive** form of breast cancer that **demands prompt recognition and treatment** to improve outcomes. Healthcare professionals play a crucial role in diagnosing and managing IBC, ensuring that patients receive individualized care. By staying informed about the latest research and treatment guidelines, healthcare providers can offer better support and enhance the quality of life for patients navigating this challenging diagnosis.

Chapter 2

ESSENTIAL CONSIDERATIONS FOR TREATMENT AND CARE

1] Metastatic Breast Cancer

Metastatic breast cancer, also known as stage **IV breast cancer**, occurs when cancer cells spread beyond the breast and nearby lymph nodes to **other parts of the body**. This progression happens when cancer cells break away from the original tumor, traveling through the bloodstream or lymphatic system to form new tumors in distant organs such as the bones, lungs, liver, or brain. Although metastatic breast cancer is **incurable**, it can be managed with ongoing treatment aimed at controlling the growth and spread of cancer cells, thus improving the patient's quality of life.

Symptoms of metastatic breast cancer **vary depending** on the location of the metastases but often include **bone pain, shortness of breath, fatigue, weight loss, and neurological issues**. It's vital for patients and healthcare professionals to work closely together to monitor any changes in symptoms or disease progression. **Early detection and timely intervention** can significantly **improve outcomes** and enhance the quality of life for patients.

Treatment for metastatic breast cancer typically involves systemic therapies such as **chemotherapy, targeted therapy, hormone therapy, or immunotherapy**. These treatments aim to target and eliminate cancer cells throughout the body. In addition, patients may receive radiation therapy or surgery to address specific symptoms or complications from metastases, such as pain or spinal cord compression. **Palliative** care is also a key component of treatment, focusing on symptom management, emotional support, and improving the overall quality of life for both patients and their families.

Healthcare professionals play a crucial role in supporting patients with metastatic breast cancer. This includes providing personalized care, educating patients about treatment options and potential side effects, and **offering emotional support throughout their journey**. Living with a terminal illness like metastatic breast cancer can evoke feelings of fear, uncertainty, and grief. Therefore, it's important for healthcare providers to address these emotional needs and connect patients with support services and resources to help them navigate the challenges of their diagnosis.

2] Hereditary Breast Cancer

Hereditary breast cancer is a type of breast cancer that arises from an **inherited gene mutation**, often leading to an increased risk of developing the disease at **a younger age** than the general population. Approximately **5-10% of all** breast cancer cases are hereditary, with the **BRCA1 and BRCA2** gene mutations being the **most commonly identified**.

For individuals with a **strong family history** of breast cancer, such as a first-degree relative diagnosed at an early age or multiple relatives affected on the same side of the family, the likelihood of hereditary breast cancer is higher. This heightened risk calls **for vigilance and proactive care**.

Recognizing the signs and symptoms of hereditary breast cancer is vital in providing appropriate care and screening for those at risk. For patients with a significant family history,

genetic testing may be recommended to identify potential gene mutations. For those who test positive, discussions about **risk-reducing strategies**, such as **prophylactic mastectomy** or **oophorectomy**, become an important part of the care plan.

It is crucial that patients with hereditary breast cancer work closely with a **specialized healthcare team**, including genetic counselors, oncologists, and surgeons. This team approach ensures that each patient receives a **personalized treatment** plan that considers their **unique genetic background** and **family history**.

Understanding hereditary breast cancer is essential for both patients and healthcare providers. **By fostering a compassionate and empathetic environment**, healthcare professionals can support individuals at higher risk, guiding them through their options with care and sensitivity. Proactive steps, informed by the latest research and genetic insights, can help reduce risk and improve quality of life for those facing hereditary breast cancer.

3] Paget's Disease of the Breast

Paget's disease of the breast **is a rare and often misunderstood** form of breast cancer. It is characterized by cancerous cells in **the skin of the nipple-areolar complex (NAC)**. This condition often **mimics common skin conditions**, presenting with symptoms such as eczema of the areola, bleeding, ulceration, and itching of the nipple. Because of its uncommon nature and the resemblance of symptoms to benign skin disorders, the diagnosis of Paget's disease is frequently delayed.

In nearly 90% of cases, Paget's disease is associated with an **underlying breast cancer**, which can be ductal carcinoma in situ (DCIS) or invasive cancer. It's important to note that this underlying cancer is not always near the NAC, which can complicate the diagnostic process.

Given the complexity of Paget's disease, it's essential for patients to work closely with their oncologist to receive an accurate diagnosis and treatment. Your oncologist will carefully evaluate your condition and recommend the best therapeutic approach to achieve the most successful outcome.

Early recognition and treatment are key, and healthcare providers play a crucial role in guiding patients through this challenging diagnosis with care and compassion. By understanding the unique aspects of Paget's disease and addressing the emotional and physical needs of patients, healthcare professionals can help navigate the journey toward recovery.

4] Cystosarcoma of Phyllodes

Cystosarcoma of phyllodes, also known simply as **phyllodes tumor, is a rare type** of breast tumor, accounting **for about 1%** of all breast neoplasms. Most of these tumors **(about 90%) are benign**, with only about **10% being malignant.** A key characteristic of phyllodes tumors is that, while **they rarely spread** (metastasize) to other parts of the body, they have a high **tendency to recur locally after treatment**. The recommended treatment for phyllodes tumors is **surgery with wide margins** to ensure all tumor tissue is removed, optimizing local control and reducing the risk of recurrence.

5] Extremely Rare Tumors: Lymphoma, Sarcoma, and Squamous Cell Carcinoma

Besides more common types of breast cancer, there are extremely rare tumors such as **lymphoma, sarcoma, and squamous cell carcinoma** that can also occur in the breast. These tumors are uncommon and require specialized treatment approaches tailored to their unique characteristics. Because of their rarity, managing these types of breast tumors often involves a multidisciplinary team of specialists to provide the most effective care.

6] Male Breast Cancer

Male breast cancer is **an uncommon** but significant health concern. Although it accounts **for less than 1%** of all breast cancer cases, **it is crucial for men** to be aware of the signs and symptoms to ensure **early detection and treatment**. Unfortunately, male breast cancer is often diagnosed at **more advanced stages** because men **are less aware** of their risk for this disease and **small size of breast**.

Several factors can increase the risk of male breast cancer, including **aging, genetic mutations, high estrogen levels**, obesity, and **liver disease**. Men with a family history of breast cancer or a **genetic predisposition** should be vigilant, as the disease can affect them at a **younger age**.

The symptoms of male breast cancer are like those of women and may include a lump or swelling in the breast, nipple discharge, or changes in the breast's skin or nipple. It's important for men to seek medical attention promptly if they notice any of these signs, as early detection is key to more effective treatment. Unfortunately, many male breast cancers are **found at a locally advanced stage**, making treatment **more challenging**.

Treatment for male breast cancer typically involves **surgery** to remove the tumor, often followed by **radiation therapy, chemotherapy, or hormone therapy**, depending on the cancer's stage and aggressiveness. Sometimes, **targeted therapies or immunotherapy** may also be part of the treatment plan.

Healthcare professionals play a crucial role in educating their male patients about the risk factors and encouraging regular self-exams. **By raising awareness and providing support**, we can help men recognize early signs of breast cancer and seek timely medical care, ultimately improving outcomes and survival rates. Understanding and addressing the unique needs of this underrepresented group is essential to providing compassionate and effective care.

Chapter 3

How Breast Cancer Affects Different Populations

Young Women with Breast Cancer

Breast cancer in young women presents **unique challenges** that differ significantly from those faced by older women. This form of cancer is often **more aggressive**, with a higher likelihood of being **hormone receptor-negative** or **triple-negative**, making treatment more complex and increasing the risk of recurrence. The risk of developing **metastatic disease** can be higher, as the bodies of young women are still in a state of growth and development.

A major concern for young women with breast cancer is the potential **impact on fertility**. Treatments such as chemotherapy can adversely affect a woman's ability to conceive in the future. It's crucial for healthcare providers to discuss **fertility preservation options** with young women at the time of diagnosis, ensuring they have the information needed to make informed decisions about their future family planning.

Beyond the physical challenges, young women with breast cancer often face **emotional and psychological struggles**. The shock and isolation that can accompany a cancer diagnosis at a young age can be overwhelming. Healthcare providers must offer robust support, including **counseling**, **support groups**, and other psychosocial resources, to help young women navigate the emotional toll of their diagnosis.

When developing treatment plans, it's important for healthcare providers to address the **unique needs and concerns** of young women. Priorities such as **preserving fertility**, maintaining **quality of life**, or **returning to work or school** must be considered alongside medical treatment options. Recognizing and respecting these concerns ensures that treatment is not only effective but also aligned with the patient's life goals.

Young women with breast cancer require **specialized care** that addresses both the medical and personal aspects of their lives. By understanding the unique challenges they face, healthcare providers can tailor treatment plans and support services to meet their specific needs. A **collaborative, compassionate approach** is essential in guiding young women through their cancer journey, helping them to navigate this hard experience with as much support and understanding as possible.

Breast Cancer in Older Women

Breast cancer can affect women at any stage of life, although the likelihood increases as women age, with most cases diagnosed in those over the age of 50. This higher susceptibility in older women brings forth distinct challenges that healthcare professionals must acknowledge and manage.

The **treatment options** and outcomes for older women with breast cancer **often differ** from those for younger women. As the **body ages, it may not tolerate** certain treatments, such as chemotherapy, as well as it once could. The risk of complications from surgery may also increase. Older women may have **other health conditions** that need to be considered when creating a treatment plan.

"It's crucial for older women to ensure **they receive regular breast cancer screenings.**" Finding the disease early can significantly improve treatment outcomes. While most women over 50 are typically advised to undergo mammograms, the frequency and timing of screenings may vary based on individual health risks. Your doctor should discuss with you the benefits and potential drawbacks of getting screened so you can make informed decisions about your health.

Older women with breast cancer not only have to cope with **physical challenges** but also may encounter **emotional** and **psychological obstacles. Feelings of loneliness, depression, or anxiety are prevalent, particularly among those who live alone or have limited social support**. It's important for healthcare providers to be mindful of these emotional needs and to offer resources and support to assist older women in addressing the emotional components of their diagnosis and treatment.

It is essential to **comprehend the intricacies** of breast cancer in older women to provide customized care. Healthcare providers must be mindful of the distinct challenges encountered by this group and collaborate closely with them to develop personalized treatment strategies that account for their age, general well-being, and specific preferences. Through the provision of **compassionate and thorough care**, healthcare professionals can enable older women with breast cancer to approach their treatment process with dignity and resilience.

Breast Cancer During Pregnancy

According to NCCN guidelines, effective communication between the **oncologist and maternal fetal** medicine specialist is crucial for every visit and therapeutic decision. A study revealed that there **were 1.3 breast cancer** cases diagnosed per **10,000 live births**. Breast cancer during pregnancy is often **LN-positive**, with a **larger primary** tumor size, **poorly differentiated** histologically, and usually **ER/PR-negative** on IHC.

During pregnancy, around **30% of breast cancer** cases are **HER2-positive. Diagnosis can be delayed** because breast **lumps may not be suspected. Mammograms with shielding** can be safely and accurately performed, with an accuracy greater than 80%. Chest X-rays with shielding are safe for early breast cancer. For advanced breast cancer, ultrasound of the liver and MRI screening of the spine can be considered, excluding metastasis.

It's important to provide **counseling for pregnant patients with breast cancer and their families**, discussing the treatment options such as mastectomy or breast-conserving surgery, and the potential utilization of systemic therapy. The prevailing surgical approach has traditionally been changed **by radical mastectomy**; however, it is workable to consider **breast-conserving** surgery **if radiation therapy can be postponed until after the pregnancy.**

It is recommended to not conduct sentinel node biopsy in pregnant patients who are less than 30 weeks into their pregnancy because of the lack of sufficient data regarding safety and dye exposure. The indications for systemic chemotherapy are comparable in pregnant and non-pregnant individuals with breast cancer. Chemotherapy should be avoided during the first trimester of pregnancy because of the heightened risk of fetal malformations.

As Per the NCCN guidelines, the likelihood of fetal malformation during the **second and third trimesters** is roughly 1.3%, which is like the risk for fetuses not exposed to chemotherapy during pregnancy. Therefore, **it is deemed safe to administer chemotherapy during these trimesters**. However, it is advisable to not administer chemotherapy after the 35th week of pregnancy or within 3 weeks of the expected delivery date to minimize the potential for hematologic complications during childbirth.

The largest experience in pregnancy has been with **anthracycline and alkylating agent chemotherapy**. Some institutions show that the **FAC regimen may be** given with **relative safety** during the second and third trimesters of pregnancy. Drugs like ondansetron, lorazepam, and dexamethasone can be used as part of the pre-chemotherapy antiemetic regimen.

Children born to mothers who received chemotherapy have shown **positive progress in terms of health and academic performance**. However, there have been reported cases of clubfoot, congenital bilateral ureteral reflux, and Down syndrome. According to the NCCN Panel, if the disease status clinically shows, **paclitaxel should be administered weekly after the first trimester.** It is strictly advised to **avoid the use of Trastuzumab** during pregnancy because of concerns related to **oligo- or anhydramnios and fetal renal failure**, which were observed in one case. Endocrine therapy and radiation therapy are **also not recommended** during pregnancy.

Chapter 4

Diagnosis and Management of Breast Cancer

Diagnosis of Breast Cancer

The process of diagnosing breast cancer requires a comprehensive approach, involving a review of medical history, physical examination, imaging tests, and tissue sampling. This requires a multidisciplinary approach. These tests may include a **mammogram, ultrasound, or MRI**, as well as **biopsies** like fine needle aspiration, core needle biopsy, or surgical biopsy. Pathology analysis plays a crucial role in identifying the specific type of breast cancer and informing treatment plans based on factors such as **hormone receptor status and HER2 status.**

Upon confirmation of a breast cancer diagnosis, additional tests may be conducted to assess the stage of the cancer, assisting in the formulation of a treatment plan. These tests may involve further imaging procedures, **such as CT scans, bone scans, or PET scans**.

Pathological classification of the tumor

Here is some information regarding tumor classification to keep in mind:

Pathological Classification of the Tumor:

When reviewing a biopsy report, you may come across various types of pathological classifications, such as:

- **Invasive ductal carcinoma (70 to 80%)**: This is the **most frequently** observed type of cancer in biopsy reports.
- Invasive **lobular** carcinoma (10% to 15%)
- Ductal or Lobular **carcinoma in situ**.
- Special **favorable histologies (<10%)**: These encompass papillary, tubular, mucinous, and pure medullary carcinomas.

Once your oncologist confirms a breast cancer diagnosis, the next crucial step involves determining the stage of the cancer. Staging is essential for understanding the extent of the cancer's spread and developing an appropriate treatment plan. The **TNM system** (Tumor size, nodal status, and Metastasis) is used to determine the stage, which may require tests such as ultrasounds, chest x-rays, CT scans, or PET scans to assess the spread of the cancer.

Based on the TNM staging, the oncologist will classify the breast cancer into one of four stages:

Stage 1

Stage 2

Stage 3

Stage 4

Treatment Options

Within the field of breast cancer treatment, a variety of options are available based on the particular type and stage of the cancer. The **primary treatment approach is multimodal**, including surgery, **radiation therapy, chemotherapy, targeted therapy, hormone therapy, precision therapy, im-**

munotherapy, and palliative care. Each of these interventions plays a crucial role in effectively addressing the illness and improving patient outcomes.

When breast cancer is detected early, the first step is usually surgery, followed by further treatment based on the tumor's specific traits, lymph node status, and overall stage. If the cancer has advanced or spread, systemic treatments like chemotherapy, targeted therapy, endocrine therapy, and Anti-HER2 therapy are usually the main options.

The primary approach for treating breast cancer typically **involves surgery**, which aims to eliminate the tumor and adjacent tissue. Various surgical options, such as lumpectomy, mastectomy, and lymph node removal, are available, and the selection of a specific procedure is determined by factors such as the size and position of the tumor, as well as the patient's general well-being and personal preferences.

Chemotherapy is treatment that makes use of potent medication to specifically target and eradicate cancerous cells throughout the body. In the realm of breast cancer care, chemotherapy is **commonly used with surgery or radiation therapy**. It can be employed **prior to surgery to shrink tumors**, following surgery to **eliminate any lin-**

gering cancer cells, or as the primary treatment where breast cancer has spread to other areas of the body.

Radiation therapy is a commonly used approach to treat breast cancer. It uses high-energy rays to eradicate cancer cells and diminish the size of tumors. Typically, this treatment is given following surgery to target any remaining cancer cells and decrease the likelihood of cancer recurrence. In certain instances, it may also be given before surgery to reduce the size of the tumors and make their removal easier.

Targeted therapy is a modern way of treating cancer that focuses on attacking cancer cells while **causing less harm** to healthy cells. It is often **used together** with other treatments for breast cancer, particularly for **HER2-positive breast cancer**. This type of therapy may involve the administration of drugs that should halt the growth of cancer cells by targeting specific genes or proteins in the body.

Hormone therapy is a highly effective treatment modality for hormone receptor-positive breast cancer (the most common type). Hormone therapy, also known as endocrine therapy, acts by blocking the effects of the hormones on the cancer cells. Hormone therapy can be used as a monotherapy treatment or in combination with other drugs to prolong survival and lower the chances of its relapse. Patients must seek guidance from their oncologist to find out the best course of action for their circumstances.

Follow-Up Care

Ongoing follow-up care after breast cancer treatment is vital for patient health. It ensures that **any signs of cancer recurrence or lasting side effects** from treatment are promptly identified. This care typically includes **regular appointments** with healthcare providers, imaging scans, blood tests, and discussions about managing any persistent symptoms or treatment-related side effects. **The schedule and duration of follow-up care are tailored** to the type and stage of breast cancer, along with the patient's specific risk factors.

"Specific patients may necessitate **more frequent** follow-up care. For example, individuals with **triple-negative breast cancer** and **young patients** with a a **strong family history** might require **intensive monitoring** because of the high risk of recurrence and the aggressive nature of the cancer. Patients with inflammatory breast cancer necessitate **closer surveillance** to ensure **early detection** of any recurrence. Those with hormone receptor-positive breast cancer may require ongoing hormone therapy and regular monitoring of hormone levels. Patients on **hormonal therapy** might encounter **bone-related** issues and may **necessitate close**

monitoring. Additionally, individuals with hereditary breast cancer could benefit from **genetic counseling** and testing for other cancer-related genetic mutations."

For patients with **metastatic breast cancer**, follow-up care focuses on managing symptoms, monitoring disease progression, and adjusting treatment plans as needed. Male breast cancer patients may require specialized follow-up care to address unique challenges and concerns. **Young women** with breast cancer may need additional support for **fertility preservation** and **long-term survivorship planning**.

"**Long-term follow-up care is essential** for breast cancer survivors to detect any delayed effects of treatment, such as issues with **heart or bone health**. Survivorship care plans are valuable tools that assist patients and healthcare providers in coordinating ongoing care and addressing any physical, emotional, or practical concerns that may arise post-treatment. By staying actively involved in follow-up care, patients can better manage their health and **ensure a good quality of life both during and after their breast cancer journey**."

CHAPTER 5

LIFE BEYOND CANCER: SUPPORT SYSTEMS AND SURVIVORSHIP

Life After Treatment

Life after treatment for breast cancer is a significant phase in a patient's journey. For many people, completing treatment marks a **major milestone, filled with both relief and celebration for overcoming the challenges faced.** This period, while joyful, also brings its own set of adjustments. Survivors may encounter a variety of physical, emotional, and psychological issues as they transition from active treatment to life as a survivor. With the right **support system**

and resilience, patients can **embrace this "second chance"** and adapt to the changes in their lives.

Once treatment is completed, a primary concern for many patients is the **fear of cancer recurrence.** To address this, maintaining open and effective communication with your oncologist is essential. During **follow-up visits**, your oncologist will conduct regular check-ups, educate you about the warning signs of recurrence, and emphasize the importance of self-examinations and clinical assessments. Regular screenings, such as **annual mammograms, are crucial**, as is active participation in community health programs. Engaging with support groups and seeking counseling can provide valuable mental, social, and emotional support, helping you cope with the fear of recurrence.

After completing treatment for breast cancer, transitioning to life as a survivor is a crucial stage in a patient's journey. It signifies a significant achievement and **evokes relief and joy for overcoming the challenges.** While this time is cause for celebration, it also requires adjustments. Survivors may experience various physical, emotional, and psychological issues as they move from active treatment to life as survivor. With the right support system and resilience, patients can embrace this "second chance" and adapt to the changes in their lives.

Oncologists have a vital role in **addressing the anxiety patients** may feel about cancer returning. It's important to encourage **open communication**, allowing patients to share their worries and receive clear, reassuring guidance. Scheduling **regular follow-up visits** and providing education on how to perform self-examinations and understand the importance of routine screenings can help patients feel more in control of their health. Recommending **participation in support groups** and counseling can **provide emotional support and coping mechanisms**, aiding patients in managing their fears and enhancing their overall well-being.

During the survivorship period, breast cancer patients may encounter a variety of changes:

1. **Physical Changes**: After completing treatment, patients may experience physical alterations such as ongoing fatigue, body aches, weight fluctuations, and lymphedema. **Fatigue can persist for months after treatment, significantly affecting quality of life.** Weight changes may occur because of treatment-related side effects, and younger women might experience early menopause, along with symptoms like hot flashes and infertility, if ovarian function has been affected by chemotherapy. **Neuropathy, or**

numbness and tingling, may develop because of certain chemotherapy drugs, which can be managed under the guidance of an oncologist. In rare cases, patients might also experience cognitive difficulties, including issues with focus and memory. **Surgical side effects like pain, tightness, or numbness around the area of mastectomy or lumpectomy, as well as restricted arm mobility, are also common.** These physical challenges can affect personal life, leading to changes in sexual desire and intimacy because of body image concerns and fatigue. **Generalized body aches are also frequently reported by patients after treatment.**

Patients are encouraged to educate themselves about managing these side effects through various strategies, including exercise, diet, and physical therapy. Consulting specialists, such as nutritionists and physical therapists, can also provide valuable support in addressing these physical challenges and enhancing overall well-being.

2. Emotional and Mental Changes: After finishing treatment, many patients may encounter **emotional and psychological difficulties**. It's common for patients to experience feelings of **depression, anxiety,** or even **post-traumatic stress**. The **fear of cancer returning** and the stress of regular check-ups can cause constant worry. Patients may also feel **uncertain about the future** and **stressed because of the financial burden** of cancer care. Some find it **challenging to return to their pre-diagnosis routines** or to adapt to a new normal, which can strain relationships with family and friends. It is essential for patients to **seek help from healthcare providers** to manage emotional distress, which may involve **counseling, medication,** or joining **support groups**. Engaging in **self-care activities, enjoying hobbies**, and finding **social support** can also play a vital role in enhancing emotional health.

3. **Social changes**: As patients navigate life after treatment, they may also face challenges related to their **relationships, work, and financial stability**. Healthcare professionals should be prepared to address these concerns and refer patients to resources that can provide help. Encouraging open communication with loved ones, employers, and financial advisors can help patients navigate these challenges and maintain a sense of normalcy in their lives.

Here are some sentences that capture the essence of life after treatment by my breast cancer patients:

Emotional and Mental Healing:

One of my patient after completing her final round of chemotherapy, she said to me that, Although the treatment had ended, the emotional scars lingered, she grappled with anxiety, relief and fear of recurrence. **She sought solace in therapy and support groups**, where sharing her experiences with fellow survivors helped her process the trauma and rebuild her mental strength. She also derived **immense gratification by helping other cancer patients** by talking to them, as she could empathise other patients.

The New Normal Life And Its Adjustments:

Another patient of mine upon enquiring about how is life after treatment, she said that after returning to her daily routine life; she had to make **subtle adjustments** to get used to her normal life. She started **cooking, active exercise, long walk, spending time with the loved ones**. These are the moments she cherished that brought her a lot of happiness. Her priorities shifted, and she embraced a **slower, more mindful pace, appreciating the beauty in everyday activities.**"

Physical Recovery and Health Monitoring

"After the final round of chemotherapy, Mrs Priti, my patient, felt a **mix of victory and tiredness**. She felt as if she was in a war against cancer and has come back home with victory. She now required **TENDER, LOVE and gentle care**. Regular follow-ups and strict monitoring with her oncologist became a part of her new routine, a constant reminder of her journey and the vigilance needed to stay cancer-free."

Body Image and Self-Confidence

One of my young breast cancer patients, Prachi, was beauty-conscious and a model by profession. After the treatment, when she looked in the mirror, she saw a body that changed her perception of beauty. She **embraced her inner beauty for happiness**. She **accepted her body the way it was**. The scars from surgery and the hair slowly growing back were visible reminders of her battle. It took time, but she learned to love her body again, celebrating its strength and resilience rather than its imperfections.

Rebuilding Relationships

Breast cancer had brought Mr. Rajesh and his family closer, but it also tested their bonds. As he recovered, he focused on nurturing these relationships, making up for lost time, and building a stronger, more supportive family unit. His journey had taught them all the importance of love and solidarity.

Career and Professional Life

Returning to work, she found that her perspective had shifted. The corporate ladder seemed less important compared to her health and happiness. She advocated for **better workplace** policies for cancer survivors, using her experience to foster a more **understanding and supportive environment** for others facing similar battles.

Pursuing Dreams and Happiness

"With a renewed lease on life, Rachel took up **painting**, a passion she had long neglected. Each brushstroke was a celebration of her survival, a way to express the emotions she couldn't put into words. Pursuing this new hobby brought joy and a sense of accomplishment, filling her days with color and creativity."

Navigating Long-Term Side Effects

"Years after her treatment, Mrs. Aditi still dealt with the lingering effects of chemotherapy. **Fatigue and neuropathy** were constant companions, but she **learned to manage them** with a combination of medication, physical therapy, and lifestyle adjustments. Her journey taught her the importance of listening to her body and **prioritizing self-care**."

Becoming an Advocate

After confronting breast cancer directly, Susan dedicated herself to advocacy for increased awareness and research. She spearheaded **community events**, including **organizing screening mammograms, hosting guest lectures, and providing guidance** to newly diagnosed patients on managing their challenges. Her personal journey equipped her with an interesting voice, and she was resolved to leverage it to create a meaningful impact in the breast cancer community.

Embracing Life and Future Planning

"Each day became a precious gift for Mrs. Leena, who embraced life with newfound purpose and enthusiasm. She began exploring the world, pursuing her dreams, and planning her future with hope and optimism. Her experience with breast cancer had imparted valuable lessons in resilience and the significance of making the most of every moment."

The above narrative highlights the diverse aspects of life following breast cancer treatment, capturing both the obstacles and victories that survivors may encounter as they adapt to their new reality.

In summary, life after breast cancer treatment can present a range of challenges for patients. It is essential for healthcare professionals to support patients through this transition by addressing physical, emotional, and practical concerns. By offering comprehensive education, resources, and emotional support, patients can adjust to life after treatment and move forward with confidence and resilience.

What patients can do during the surivorship period to make their life better?

Embrace a Healthy Lifestyle: Incorporate nutritious eating habits, engage in consistent physical activity, and work to manage weight effectively. This proactive approach helps in maintaining overall health.

Foster Positive Relationships: Build and maintain supportive connections with loved ones and peers, which can contribute to a positive and encouraging environment.

Maintain a Positive Outlook: attempt to smile and find joy in daily experiences. A cheerful attitude can positively affect emotional well-being.

Travel and Explore: Take advantage of opportunities to visit new destinations, which can offer fresh experiences and broaden your perspective on life.

Anticipate and Prepare: Identify potential challenges in advance and implement preventive measures to manage them proactively.

Adapt to New Circumstances: Navigate the transition to life after treatment by establishing a new routine that accommodates your current situation.

Reevaluate Goals and Priorities: Reflect on your life's goals and purpose to align them with your post-treatment reality and aspirations.

Take part in Support Networks: Engage with support groups and advocacy organizations to connect with others and contribute to the broader community.

Be a Source of inspiration: Use your journey and experiences to motivate and support others facing similar challenges.

Coping Strategies

A diagnosis of breast cancer can be **distressing and emotional for both patients and their families**. Healthcare professionals must offer **comprehensive support** to cope with **emotional, physical, mental, social, and financial challenges**. Effective coping mechanisms are vital for helping patients through their treatment journey and enhancing their quality of life.

A valuable strategy for coping with breast cancer involves **reaching out to family, friends, and support groups**. Connecting with people who have faced similar experiences can offer much-needed emotional support and reassurance. Support groups can help to provide both comfort and practical advice on managing treatment side effects and emotional stress. Healthcare providers should encourage patients to engage with their **support networks and explore support group** options to aid in managing their condition effectively.

Key strategies for managing breast cancer effectively include:

1. Embracing a healthy lifestyle.
2. Following a balanced diet.
3. Engaging in regular physical activity.
4. Practicing stress-relief techniques like yoga and meditation.

It's also essential for patients to communicate openly with their oncologist about any concerns or fears they may have. Oncologists should foster a supportive environment where patients feel at ease discussing their emotions and asking questions about their treatment. By encouraging patients to actively participate in their care, they can feel more empowered to manage their diagnosis and make informed decisions about their treatment options.

For patients experiencing significant emotional distress, consulting a counselor or therapist can be incredibly helpful. Healthcare providers should recognize the mental strain that a breast cancer diagnosis can bring and direct patients to appropriate mental health services when needed. Counseling can assist patients in understanding their emotions, developing coping strategies, and enhancing their mental resilience during and after treatment.

Ultimately, managing a breast cancer diagnosis is a deeply personal journey that requires **patience, resilience, and support**. Healthcare professionals help to help patients through this challenging period, providing them with crucial tools and resources for effective coping. By embracing these coping **strategies and fostering collaboration**, patients, healthcare providers, and support networks can work together to help individuals with breast cancer lead fulfilling lives despite their diagnosis.

With strategies like these to build resilience, you'll transform from your breast cancer journey like a **butterfly emerging from its chrysalis**. These coping skills will become integral to your renewed identity—a powerful advocate of life's challenges. You'll develop into a person of insight, courage, and wisdom, where "surviving" is just the beginning of truly thriving.

Support resources

Access to support resources can profoundly affect the journey of those battling breast cancer. Regardless of whether you are a doctor, nurse, patient, medical student, or healthcare professional, familiarity with the various support options available is crucial for offering comprehensive care. These resources range from emotional support to practical help and are essential for navigating the complexities of diagnosis, treatment, and survivorship.

Breast cancer support groups are invaluable resources for those affected by the disease. These gatherings create a **supportive environment** where patients can **openly discuss their experiences, apprehensions, and worries** with fellow individuals facing similar challenges. By fostering connections with others who comprehend their situation, patients often **discover solace, resilience, and motivation** to confront the difficulties ahead.

These support networks offer various benefits:

Emotional assistance: Interacting with others who truly grasp the situation can ease feelings of solitude and distress.

Practical insights: Participants frequently exchange advice on handling treatment side effects, dealing with healthcare systems, and addressing everyday hurdles.

Knowledge exchange: Members can learn about emerging treatments, ongoing clinical studies, or local support services from their peers.

Increased confidence: Hearing success stories from others can instill hope and encourage individuals to persevere through their own journey.

Adaptive techniques: Participants can gain diverse methods for managing stress, enhancing family communication, and maintaining an optimistic perspective.

Community bonds: The group often evolves into a source of companionship and belonging during challenging times.

Support groups are available in **both in-person and online formats**, catering to different preferences and needs. In-person meetings facilitate direct interaction and immediate emotional connections, while online platforms offer convenience, accessibility, and potentially broader geographical reach.

Another essential resource for individuals with breast cancer is **counseling services**. Facing a cancer diagnosis can be emotionally taxing, and counseling offers a supportive space for patients to explore their feelings, fears, and worries. **Professional counselors help** develop coping mechanisms, managing stress, and enhancing overall mental health. These counseling services are available through hospitals, cancer centers, and community organizations focused on cancer support. survivorship

For patients requiring practical help, several support resources are available to assist with **everyday tasks, transportation** to medical appointments, and financial challenges. Various organizations and **local cancer charities provide programs and services designed to support individuals** with breast cancer. These resources can offer crucial aid in navigating the healthcare system, accessing treatment options, and managing the financial aspects of cancer care.

Beyond support groups, counseling, and practical aid, educational resources are crucial for individuals with breast cancer. These resources offer valuable insights into their diagnosis, available treatment options, and potential side effects. Through **informational materials, workshops, and seminars**, patients can become better informed and make more empowered decisions about their care. Being well-versed in breast cancer allows patients to actively take part in their treatment process and advocate effectively for their health.

CHAPTER 6

HEALTHCARE PROFESSIONALS ROLE IN BREAST CANCER CARE

Screening and diagnosis

Screening and diagnosis are **crucial steps in the early detection and management** of breast cancer. Regular screening is recommended for all women, especially those at **higher risk** because of factors such **as age, family history, or genetic predisposition. Mammograms are the most common screening tool** used to detect breast cancer in its early stages. These X-ray images can help identify tumors or other abnormalities that may show cancer.

Besides mammograms, other screening methods, such as clinical breast exams and breast self-exams, are also important for detecting breast cancer early. Doctors and nurses play a critical role in educating patients on the importance of regular screenings and self-exams, as well as in performing thorough clinical exams to detect any signs of breast cancer. For medical students and healthcare professionals, understanding the various screening methods and diagnostic tools available is essential for effectively identifying and diagnosing breast cancer in patients.

Once a potential abnormality is detected through screening, further diagnostic tests may be recommended to confirm breast cancer. These tests may include **breast ultrasound, MRI, or biopsy** procedures to analyze tissue samples for cancer cells. It is important for healthcare professionals to carefully interpret the results and communicate them clearly to patients, providing support and guidance throughout the diagnostic process.

For patients diagnosed with breast cancer, understanding the **specific subtype of their cancer is crucial** for determining the most **effective treatment plan**. Different breast cancer, such as **triple negative, hormone receptor-positive, or inflammatory breast cance**r, may require **different approaches** to treatment. Healthcare professionals must work closely with patients to develop personalized treatment plans that consider the unique characteristics of their cancer and their overall health.

In conclusion, **screening and diagnosis are essential components** of breast cancer care that require collaboration between healthcare professionals and patients. By staying informed about the **latest screening guidelines and diagnostic tools,** doctors, nurses, and medical students can help ensure early detection and timely treatment of breast cancer. For patients, being **proactive about regular screenings and self-exams** can help detect **breast cancer in its early stages**, improving the chances of **successful treatment and recovery**.

CHAPTER 7

PATIENT VOICES: STORIES AND INSIGHTS

Stories of Hope and Resilience

This section **pays tribute to the incredible journeys** of individuals who have faced breast cancer with steadfast courage and resilience. Their stories stand as powerful **symbols of hope and inspiration** for patients, healthcare providers, and everyone affected by this disease. These accounts highlight the **extraordinary strength and determination** shown by those navigating the hard path of a breast cancer diagnosis.

One such story is that of **Mrs Reshma,** a **young woman diagnosed** with **triple negative breast cancer** at 30. Despite the aggressive nature of her cancer, Emily remained positive and hopeful throughout her treatment. With the support of her healthcare team and loved ones, she completed chemotherapy and radiation therapy, and is now cancer-free. Mrs Reshma's story serves as a reminder that with sheer determination and a positive attitude, it is possible to overcome even the most challenging obstacles.

Another inspiring story comes from **Mrs Prachi**, a survivor of **inflammatory breast cancer**. Despite the **rarity and aggressive nature of her diagnosis,** Prachi refused to let her cancer define her. Through many rounds of chemotherapy and a mastectomy, Prachi remained strong. Today, she is an advocate for breast cancer awareness and a source of inspiration for other women facing similar challenges.

Another remarkable account is that of a **45-year-old man named Adil,** who received an unexpected breast cancer diagnosis. Like many, Adil was unaware that this disease could affect men, making his initial reaction was one of disbelief. However, he swiftly overcame his shock and approached his treatment with remarkable bravery and determination. Adil's treatment plan included surgical intervention, chemotherapy and hormone therapy, all of which he underwent with unwavering resolve. His perseverance paid off, and he successfully overcame his cancer.

Emphasizes the need for inclusive **education and screening practices**. His narrative not only inspires those facing similar challenges but also educates the broader public about the diverse faces of breast cancer.

These stories shine a light on the incredible resilience and strength displayed by those who face the challenges of breast cancer. They show that while the journey is tough, with the right support, determination, and medical care, it is possible to overcome even the most daunting obstacles.

Sharing these personal experiences **brings comfort** and **hope to others** who are currently battling breast cancer. These narratives serve as a reminder that they are not alone, and that others have walked the same path and come out stronger.

Besides **providing emotional support**, these stories play a vital role in **increasing awareness** of breast cancer. They help to **break down misconceptions**, promote a deeper understanding of the disease, and stress the importance of early detection and treatment. By **encouraging open discussions,** we can inspire more people to take charge of their health.

The goal of sharing these experiences is to **build a community that is united in the fight against breast cancer**.

Through increased awareness and mutual support, we can work towards a future where breast cancer is more effectively managed, or even prevented altogether.

By combining the power of personal stories with advancements in research and treatment, we edge closer to a world where breast cancer no longer poses a significant threat. Until that day comes, these stories of courage and resilience stand as powerful reminders of the strength that lies within each of us.

Advocacy and Awareness

Advocacy and awareness are **vital in the battle against breast cancer**. As healthcare professionals, we have a duty to support our patients' needs and to spread awareness about the significance of early detection, available treatment options, and the support services that can assist those affected. By actively advocating for our patients and raising our voices, we can empower them to make well-informed decisions about their healthcare, ultimately enhancing their quality of life.

Awareness and advocacy play vital roles in empowering breast cancer patients and improving overall outcomes. Here's a rephrased version of the key points:

Patients who **actively engage with their breast cancer diagnosis** often experience **better results**. By seeking knowledge about their condition and exploring treatment possibilities, they can take part more effectively in their own care decisions. This informed approach allows patients to work collaboratively with their healthcare team, potentially leading to more personalized and effective treatment plans.

Beyond personal benefit, patients **who share their experiences contribute to broader community awareness. This grassroots advocacy can**:

1. Reduce stigma surrounding breast cancer
2. Increase public understanding of the disease
3. Improve access to essential support services and resources
4. Motivate others to prioritize breast health through regular screenings and self-examinations

By raising their voices, patients become powerful agents of change. They can **influence public policy, research priorities, and healthcare practices**. This advocacy not only benefits current patients but also paves the way for better care and support for future individuals affected by breast cancer.

Increased awareness often leads to earlier detection, which is crucial for **improving survival rates and treatment outcomes**. By **encouraging open discussions** about breast health, advocates help create an environment where people feel comfortable seeking medical attention for any concerns.

Advocacy and awareness are indeed essential across the diverse spectrum of breast cancer experiences.

Each subgroup faces unique challenges that require targeted attention and support.

The **landscape of breast cancer is diverse**, encompassing various subtypes and affecting different demographic groups in distinct ways. **Advocacy efforts need to address** the specific needs of each group:

1. **Aggressive Breast cancers**: Breast cancers like triple-negative and inflammatory breast cancers and Her-2 neu subtypes require more research and personalized treatment approaches.

2. **Hormone-sensitive cancers**: Patients with hormone receptor-positive breast cancer benefit from advocacy for continued research into endocrine therapy, endocrine resistance because of various mu-

tations, and understanding the emerging mutations and their targeted therapies.

3. **Genetic predisposition**: Patients with hereditary breast cancer should be encouraged for genetic counseling and prophylactic measures.

4. **Advanced disease**: Metastatic breast cancer patients require advocacy for better treatment options and quality of life. This improves the outcomes in terms of progression-free survival and overall survival.

5. **Gender considerations**: Male breast cancer awareness is crucial to ensure timely diagnosis and care.

6. **Age-specific issues**: Young women with breast cancer face unique challenges related to fertility and long-term survivorship, while older women may have different treatment considerations.

7. **Racial disparities:** African American women experience disproportionate mortality rates, highlighting the need for targeted interventions and research.

8. **Survivorship:** Long-term survivors require ongoing support and monitoring for late effects of treatment.

Advocacy efforts in these areas can drive progress by:

1. Promoting increased funding for targeted research
2. Enhancing access to state-of-the-art screening and treatment modalities
3. Developing customized support services for specific populations
4. Addressing healthcare disparities
5. Educating healthcare providers and the public about the diverse faces of breast cancer

By recognizing and addressing these varied challenges, we can work towards more fair and effective care for all individuals affected by breast cancer.

To sum up, **the roles of advocacy and awareness are fundamental** in our **collective efforts against breast cancer**. These elements form the backbone of progress in patient care, research, and support systems.

By uniting as a healthcare community, we can:

1. Elevate public understanding of breast cancer

2. Enhance support networks for patients and their loved ones

3. Champion improved care standards and resource allocation

Our continued emphasis on these areas can yield significant positive outcomes for those affected by breast cancer. This concerted effort has the potential to transform lives, offering hope and practical help to patients and their families.

As we look ahead, let's reaffirm our commitment to advocacy and awareness. These tools are instrumental in our ongoing battle against breast cancer. Through persistent effort and collaboration, we move closer to a future where breast cancer's impact on our communities is dramatically reduced.

By maintaining this focus, we contribute to a world where breast cancer is better understood, more effectively treated, and ultimately less prevalent. This vision drives our continued dedication to advocacy and awareness in all aspects of breast cancer care and research.

Empowering Patients

Promoting patient autonomy is fundamental in addressing breast cancer effectively. **Medical professionals** bear the responsibility of **equipping individuals with vital knowledge and resources**, enabling them to become **active participants** in their healthcare journey. By fostering an environment of **patient empowerment**, we facilitate a deeper comprehension of the **intricacies involved in breast cancer management** and encourage **well-informed choices**. This strategy not only **enhances the overall quality of care** but also **instills a sense of agency and resilience** in patients as they confront their diagnosis. An **empowered individual** is better equipped to engage meaningfully with their **treatment regimen**, adapt to challenges, and work towards the **best possible health outcomes**. Ultimately, this approach transforms patients from **passive recipients of care** into **proactive partners** in their own healing process.

Patient empowerment is rooted in **comprehensive education**. Providing individuals with **precise, up-to-date, and easily digestible information** about their breast cancer diagnosis, available treatment modalities, and possible adverse effects is crucial. This **knowledge base** equips patients to **grasp the nuances of their condition** more fully. Armed with this understanding, individuals can take part more actively in their **care decisions**, making choices that align with their **values and preferences**. This **informed stance** bolsters patients' **self-advocacy skills**, enabling them to **voice their concerns and needs** more confidently. **Enhanced patient knowledge** also facilitates more **productive dialogues** with healthcare providers, fostering a **partnership approach to care**. This **collaborative dynamic** often results in **treatment plans** that are not only more tailored to the individual but also more likely to be followed, potentially improving overall outcomes.

Another important aspect of **empowering patients** is encouraging them to take an **active role in their treatment**. This can involve **setting goals** for their care, **asking questions** about their treatment plan, and **taking part in shared decision-making** with their healthcare team. By involving patients in their care, we can help them **feel more in control of their health** and **improve their overall experience** with treatment.

Empowering patients goes beyond medical education to include **comprehensive psychosocial support**. This approach connects patients to **mental health services**, **peer support**, and **holistic wellness resources**, helping them develop **coping strategies** and **resilience**. Addressing the

emotional impact of a breast cancer diagnosis is crucial for **guiding patients through treatment with confidence**.

Patient empowerment is foundational to **quality breast cancer care**, requiring a strategy that integrates **health education**, **active participation in care decisions**, and strong **psychosocial support**. By equipping patients with the tools to **manage their condition**, healthcare professionals enhance **patient outcomes** and contribute to more **responsive, patient-centered care practices.**

Chapter 8

What's Next: Advancements in Breast Cancer Research

Emerging Therapies

Recent advancements in breast cancer treatment have introduced a range of innovative therapies, offering new possibilities for both patients and healthcare professionals. These **cutting-edge approaches**, including **targeted therapies** and **immunotherapy**, present exciting opportunities for managing the disease more effectively. With these emerging options, there is renewed hope for improving patient outcomes and enhancing the overall efficacy of breast cancer treatment.

Precision oncology has revolutionized breast cancer treatment through the development of targeted therapies. These innovative interventions focus on specific molecular abnormalities within cancer cells, aiming to disrupt tumor growth while sparing healthy tissue. By zeroing in on aberrant cellular pathways, these treatments offer a more **refined approach** compared to conventional therapies.

Targeted agents have shown particular efficacy in managing several breast cancer subtypes. For tumors expressing hormone receptors, endocrine-targeted treatments have proven valuable. HER2-positive cancers often respond well to therapies designed to block HER2 signaling. In cases involving BRCA mutations, drugs targeting DNA repair mechanisms have emerged as promising options.

This approach exemplifies the **shift towards personalized medicine in oncology**, potentially improving treatment outcomes while minimizing adverse effects. As research progresses, targeted therapies continue to expand the arsenal against breast cancer, offering hope for more effective and tailored treatment strategies.

Immunotherapeutic approaches are emerging as a promising frontier in breast cancer management. This innovative strategy aims to bolster the body's inherent immune defenses against malignant cells. **By recalibrating immune responses**, these treatments seek to enhance tumor recognition and eradication.

While still in early developmental stages for breast cancer, **immunotherapy** has shown encouraging results in preliminary studies, particularly for **aggressive subtypes like triple-negative** breast cancer. This method represents a shift from conventional treatments, focusing instead on harnessing the immune system's potential to combat cancer.

As a potential adjunct to established therapies, **immunotherapy may synergize with existing treatment modalities**. Ongoing research aims to optimize its efficacy and identify suitable patient populations. As our grasp of cancer immunology advances, this approach could become an integral component of comprehensive breast cancer care, offering new avenues for treatment.

Besides targeted therapies and immunotherapy, emerging treatments for breast cancer include **personalized medicine and gene therapy**. Personalized medicine tailors treatment based on a patient's unique genetic profile and cancer characteristics, allowing for more effective strategies by targeting specific genetic mutations. **Gene therapy**, though still experimental, introduces genetic material into cancer cells to enhance their ability to fight the disease.

The field of breast cancer treatment **is rapidly advancing**, with **new therapies and approaches** being continuously developed and evaluated. It is vital for healthcare professionals to stay current with these innovations to ensure optimal patient care. By being aware of the latest progress, doctors, nurses, and other healthcare providers can improve treatment outcomes and further the fight against breast cancer.

Precision Medicine

Precision medicine **revolutionizes healthcare by customizing** treatments based on individual patients' genetic profiles, environmental factors, and lifestyles. In breast cancer care, this approach enables oncologists to **pinpoint specific genetic** alterations driving tumor growth. By developing targeted therapies for these mutations, medical teams can enhance treatment efficacy while minimizing adverse effects typically associated with conventional cancer therapies. This personalized strategy aims to **improve patient outcomes through tailored interventions** that address the unique characteristics of each patient's cancer.

One of the key advances in precision medicine for breast cancer is the **development of targeted therapies** that specifically **attack the molecular pathways** involved in cancer growth. These targeted therapies, such **as HER2 inhibitors and PARP** inhibitors, have revolutionized the treatment of breast cancer by providing **more effective and less toxic** options for patients with specific types of the disease. By identifying the genetic mutations driving a patient's cancer, healthcare professionals can choose the most appropriate targeted therapy to attack the cancer at its source.

Besides targeted therapies, **precision medicine leverages predictive biomarkers** to inform treatment strategies. These molecular indicators, detectable in various biological samples, can reveal disease status or expect therapeutic responses. **Analyzing a patient's tumor biomarkers** enables healthcare providers to design tailored treatment regimens, aiming to maximize efficacy and minimize adverse reactions. This data-driven approach enhances clinical decision-making, allowing for a more individualized and potentially more effective cancer management plan.

The landscape of precision medicine is in constant flux, with **innovations in technology and treatment methodologies emerging at a rapid pace**. For those battling breast cancer, this developing field offers hope through increasingly personalized and potent therapeutic options, potentially improving both survival rates and patient well-being. Engaging with healthcare **experts specializing in precision oncology allows patients to access state-of-the-art cancer management techniques**. This collaboration results in bespoke treatment strategies that align closely with each individual's unique medical circumstances, marking a significant shift towards more targeted and potentially more successful cancer care approaches.

Precision medicine is **transforming breast cancer treatment**, offering **tailored therapies** that surpass traditional methods in both efficacy and reduced toxicity. **By pinpointing cancer-driving genetic alterations** and using predictive biomarkers, healthcare teams can enhance patient outcomes and life quality. As this field progresses, it's crucial for the entire medical community - from patients to seasoned professionals - to stay abreast of recent developments. This ongoing education ensures the delivery of optimal, groundbreaking care for those battling breast cancer. The future of oncology lies in this personalized approach, promising more effective and individualized treatment strategies.

Preventive Strategies

Minimizing breast cancer risk hinges on effective prevention strategies, with health practitioners acting as crucial information conduits for their patients. By comprehending these preventive approaches, individuals can actively take part in their health management and make well-informed lifestyle choices.

A cornerstone of prevention revolves around **maintaining optimal body composition**, achieved through **mindful eating and regular physical engagement**. Research findings show a connection between elevated body mass and heightened susceptibility to hormone-influenced breast malignancies. Healthcare experts can significantly affect patient outcomes by advocating for **nutrient-rich dietary** choices and **consistent exercise regimens**. This guidance equips patients with practical tools to potentially reduce their vulnerability to this specific breast cancer variant, fostering a proactive stance towards long-term wellness.

Limiting alcohol intake is a key preventive measure against breast cancer. Studies link alcohol consumption to higher breast cancer risk, especially hormone-sensitive types. Healthcare providers should advise patients, particularly those at elevated risk, to reduce alcohol consumption as a protective strategy.

For those with familial breast cancer history or known **genetic risks, genetic counseling and testing offer** valuable preventive insights. This approach enables medical professionals to **identify high-risk individuals** and recommend **customized screening and risk-reduction plans**. These targeted interventions aim to decrease breast cancer likelihood in susceptible patients.

These strategies, coupled with patient education and regular medical supervision, create a robust framework for breast cancer prevention. By promoting these approaches, healthcare teams enable patients to proactively manage their breast cancer risk.

Routine breast cancer screenings, encompassing mammography and clinical assessments, are vital for early detection. Timely diagnosis markedly improves treatment outcomes and survival prospects. Medical professionals should guide patients on personalized screening schedules, considering **factors like age and familial risk**.

Breast cancer prevention hinges on a multi-faceted approach. By **promoting wellness-focused habits**, facilitating genetic risk assessments when relevant, and underscoring the value of systematic screenings, healthcare teams empower patients to actively mitigate their breast cancer risk. **This synergistic effort between medical experts and individuals** is crucial in enhancing health outcomes for those susceptible to breast cancer.

CONCLUSION AND RESOURCES

Summary of Key Points

In this subchapter, we have covered a range of key points related to breast cancer, including different breast cancer, risk factors, treatment options, and support resources for patients and healthcare professionals.

Foremost, it is important to **understand the different breast cancer, such as Her2 positive breast cancer, triple negative breast cancer, inflammatory breast cancer, hormone receptor-positive breast cancer,** hereditary breast cancer, and metastatic breast cancer. Each type of breast cancer has its own unique characteristics and treatment options, so it is crucial to accurately diagnose and classify the type of breast cancer in order to develop an effective treatment plan.

We have **discussed various risk factors** for breast cancer, including genetic predisposition, age, gender, and lifestyle factors. By understanding these risk factors, healthcare professionals can better assess a patient's likelihood of developing breast cancer and provide screening and prevention strategies.

Early detection and treatment of breast cancer are of paramount importance in giving the best chance of a cure to the patients. Breast cancer screening tests, such as mammograms and clinical breast exams, can detect breast cancer at an early stage. Treatment options for breast cancer may include surgery, chemotherapy, hormone therapy, and targeted therapy. Radiation therapy is also a part of the treatment plan during the journey of treatment. Overall treatment plans depend on the type and stage of the cancer.

Last, we have emphasized the **importance of providing comprehensive support for patients** with breast cancer, including access to **counseling, support groups, and resources** for managing treatment side effects and coping with the emotional impact of a breast cancer diagnosis. **By working together**, patients can get the best possible care and improve their quality of life throughout their cancer journey.

Additional Reading and Support Groups

Patients suffering from breast cancer should look for **support groups** and **reading materials** that can provide valuable resources for the best possible care. Support groups **offer mental, financial, and emotional support** to the patients. They also provide practical advice and a sense of community for those affected by the disease. Patients can benefit by sharing their experiences with others who understand what they are going through. The support groups allow individuals to share their journeys and experiences, fostering a unique sense of empathy and understanding. The support groups also provide personalized information that addresses the unique challenges faced by breast cancer survivors.

Support groups for patients with breast cancer are available. This includes **in-person physical meetings, social media platforms, online discussion forums, and telephone helplines**. These groups may be mentored by healthcare professionals, social workers, or community leaders who can provide information and guidance on coping with the emotional and physical challenges of breast cancer. Support groups also help **to build a powerful community of survivors** who support and uplift each other. Support groups can also help patients to **access resources and make an informed decision**.

Breast cancer patients can access various help educational resources to expand their understanding and develop coping strategies. These include **books, online articles, and specialized websites** offering crucial information on the disease, treatments, and **post-diagnosis life**. Such resources help patients better comprehend their condition, take part in treatment decisions, and address the multifaceted challenges of breast cancer.

Support groups play a vital role in patients' well-being by:

1. Emotional Support:

- Providing psychological help

- Offering a safe space for emotional expression

- Promoting mental health

2. Inspiration:

- Sharing success stories of cancer survivors

- Offering role models for newly diagnosed patients

3. Practical Advice:

- Exchanging tips for managing treatment side effects

- Sharing strategies for lifestyle adjustments

4. Resource Sharing:

- Serving as an information hub for medical, financial, and emotional support services

5. Ongoing Care:

- Ensuring continuous support throughout the cancer journey

6. Skill Enhancement:

- Organizing activities to build coping skills

- Hosting workshops on stress management and overall well-being

7. Life Quality Improvement:

- Encouraging positive thinking

- Creating a supportive environment

- Providing comprehensive care

By staying informed, healthcare professionals can provide the best possible care for their patients and help them achieve the best possible outcomes. Healthcare professionals can use reading materials to educate their patients about their diagnosis, treatment options, and survivorship, empowering them to make informed decisions about their care.

Overall, **support groups and additional reading materials** can be valuable resources for patients and healthcare professionals working with breast cancer. By participating in support groups and educating themselves through reading materials, patients and healthcare professionals can better cope with the challenges of breast cancer, stay informed about the latest research and treatment options, and ultimately improve outcomes for those affected by the disease.

How to Stay Informed and Involved

Patients should take an **active role in their healthcare** by continuously seeking and staying updated with **the latest information**. This proactive approach empowers them to navigate their journey with confidence and make well-informed decisions. Keeping up with new research, treatment advancements, and available support systems is essential.

It's crucial to fully **understand your diagnosis, treatment options, stages, and overall prognosis**. Engaging in regular discussions with your oncologist, asking specific questions, conducting your own research, and connecting with support groups can enhance your understanding and guide your choices. Being informed also strengthens communication with your healthcare team.

Patients should **actively seek mentorship, find sources of inspiration, and engage in social activities.** These steps can help boost confidence and resilience, making it easier to face challenges. By learning from others who have experienced similar situations, patients can better equip themselves for the journey ahead.

As we wrap up this journey, the fight against breast cancer is a **combined effort involving patients, healthcare providers, and the community**. When everyone works together, shares knowledge, and provides heartfelt support, we may ensure that each person receives the best care they deserve. Let us also embrace hope and determination, which can make a meaningful difference in each person's battle with breast cancer. **Together, we have the strength to inspire, uplift, and positively impact lives.**

REFERENCES

1. NCCN Guidelines 2024

2. ESMO Guidelines 2024

3. Devita Textbook of Oncology

4. ASCO guidelines 2024

5. NICE Guidelines

6. www. Breastcancer.org

7. www.cancer.org

DISCLAIMER

This book is for educational purposes only. Readers acknowledge that the author does not render legal, financial, medical, or professional advice. The content within this book has been derived from various sources. Please consult a licensed professional before attempting any techniques outlined in this book.

By reading this document, the reader agrees that under no circumstances is the author responsible for any direct or indirect losses incurred as a result of the use of the information contained within this document, including but not limited to errors, omissions, or inaccuracies.

Adherence to all applicable laws and regulations, including international, federal, state, and local governing professional licensing, business practices, advertising, and all other jurisdictions, is the sole responsibility of the purchaser or reader.

Neither the author nor the publisher assumes any responsibility or liability whatsoever on behalf of the purchaser or reader of these materials. Any perceived slight of any individual or organization is purely unintentional.

www.ingramcontent.com/pod-product-compliance
Lightning Source LLC
LaVergne TN
LVHW091117150826
845673LV00002B/866

* 9 7 9 8 8 9 5 8 8 0 1 8 0 *